MW00438180

CONTENTS

THE SPIRITUAL WARFARE

THE
SPIRITUAL WARFARE

By

JESSIE PENN-LEWIS

CHRISTIAN • LITERATURE • CRUSADE
Fort Washington, Pennsylvania 19034

CHRISTIAN LITERATURE CRUSADE

U.S.A.
Box 1449, Fort Washington, Pa. 19034

GREAT BRITAIN
51 The Dean, Alresford, Hants. SO24 9BJ

Originally published by
THE OVERCOMER LITERATURE TRUST
England

First American edition
1989
Revised 1991

ISBN 0-87508-962-3

Scripture quotations from:
The King James Version unless otherwise
indicated.
The American Standard Version (ASV),
1901, Thomas Nelson & Sons, New York.
The Epistles of Paul (a translation and notes)
by W. J. Conybeare, England (died 1857).
The New Testament in Modern Speech,
R. F. Weymouth, 1903, 1924, England.

Printed in Colombia

CHAPTER 1

THE SPIRITUAL WARFARE

"Put on the whole armour of God, that you may be able to stand firm against the wiles of the Devil. For the adversaries with whom we wrestle . . . are the Principalities, the Powers, and the Sovereigns of this present darkness, the spirits of evil in the heavens" (Ephesians 6:11–12, *Conybeare*).

WE wonder if the Lord's people really believe that the Bible means exactly what it says, when it is written that the "whole world lieth in the evil one," and that the "prince of the power of the air" is the spirit that now works in the sons of disobedience! Moreover, that Satan is the god of this world, and that his principalities and powers are the *world-rulers* of this darkness? *Apart from the death of Christ* as an expiatory sacrifice for sin, and the recognition of the death of the sinner with the Saviour, there is no guarantee of any soul not being misled by the Adversary—not even *righteousness* being a sufficient safeguard, as we see in 2 Corinthians 11:15. Do we believe that?

The dividing line of the cross has become acute in

Christendom. Through the acceptance of the cross the sons of God are being ripened for translation; and through the rejection of the cross the children of unbelief will be left in darkness—a darkness none the less dark because it is termed "light," and "progress."

There is a sphere of prayer which lies beyond the simple asking for "blessing"—a sphere of prayer opened out in Ephesians 6, and known only by those who have experientially passed, *on the basis of Romans 6,* and by way of Ephesians 1, 2, 3, 4, and 5, on to the sixth chapter. This sphere involves warfare!

The pivot verse in Romans 6 is "*Knowing* this, that our old man was *crucified with Him.*" Then in Ephesians 1 and 2, Paul shows how Christ was raised from the dead, and we were *raised up together with Him,* and made to *sit with Him* in the heavenly places in Christ. Finally Ephesians 6 shows the spiritual *conflict* with spirit foes, which the believer finds himself brought into *as he really experiences spirit-union with Christ.*

In *union* with the enthroned Lord, the believer in due time finds the conflict of Ephesians 6 open to him, and discovers that there is a *prayer-warfare* where he not only needs Christ as his life within but also as "the whole armour of God," his covering without. Here he will meet in direct combat, without any intervention of "flesh and blood," the satanic principalities and powers, and learn, by standing on the firm foundation of the gospel (e.g., *Christ crucified*) to overthrow the foe— and then with "unwearied persistence" to *hold the victory* for himself and others, especially for messengers going forth to proclaim the Good News. Hallelujah!

CHAPTER 2

WHAT IS "PRAYER WARFARE"?

BRIEFLY, prayer warfare simply means holding unceasingly the power of the "finished work of Christ" over the hosts of evil, in their attack upon some place or person, until the victory is won. Just as Moses lifted his hands stedfastly until the victory was won, so the prayer warrior holds up stedfastly the victory of the cross—the finished victory of Christ over Satan—until the forces of evil retreat and are vanquished.

This requires a true knowledge of Romans 6 and Galatians 2:20 in experience, and many lessons on abiding on the throne with Christ (Ephesians 2:6), before prolonged conflicts are thus prayed through and won. The truth is, so many believers live in inward conflict regarding themselves that they cannot understand Ephesians 6 with its warfare against spiritual hosts of evil in the atmosphere where, *"Christ-encased,"* the prayer warriors wrestle and overthrow the principalities and powers attacking the church of Christ.

"Prayer warfare" has to do entirely with direct warfare with the powers of darkness—not with "flesh and blood" (Ephesians 6:12); therefore it does not admit the exercise of "will power" (or psychic force), for if such warfare is needed in connection with persons, it is *not with the individual himself* but with the adversary who is blinding him, or misleading him, that we "wrestle." Let prayer warriors claim the "It is finished" of Calvary upon the unseen hosts of Satan opposing the proclamation of the gospel, or holding souls in bondage and darkness. Christ's last words of triumph will prevail, as we pray through in union with Him on the throne.

CHAPTER 3

THE WAY INTO THE "WARFARE" PLANE

THE warfare plane is on the resurrection side of the cross, not in the earth sphere. It is when the spirit is set free, and united to the risen Christ, that we come up against the evil powers in the atmosphere. The taking of your position on the basis of Romans 6 needs to be understood as the foundation of the growth of the spiritual life, and all the advance from plane to plane which follows. Just as you saw that Christ bore your sins in His own body on the tree, and when you believed this, God gave you a new life, so you see that the old creation—the old Adam—was also taken by Him to the cross; i.e., (1) as you hold the position that all the guilt of sin has been put away, so you hold the position that (2) the "old Adam" in entirety has been nailed to the cross. Both call for a "reckoning" of faith which God makes true. In the first instance *sins* are put away; in the second instance you are put into a position in which you may have victory over *sin*.

As you hold that position or attitude toward sin, you find sin loses its power to hold you. The "warfare plane" of Ephesians 6 is not a fight with *sin,* but the conflict of the new creation with *spirit foes* while the believer holds steadily his *death attitude toward sin.*

For the victory of *Ephesians 6* the believer must therefore hold the foundation of *Romans 6* very clearly, for if the "old Adam" life is allowed to intervene, it is certain defeat on the "warfare plane."

But if you have the death of the cross in its aspect of the "old man" crucified really wrought into you by the Holy Spirit, some force against sin rises up in you enabling you to say, "I *will* not," instead of being helplessly overcome. Because Christ did this work on the cross, no sin has a *right* to dominion over you. If you *will not* let sin reign, the word is clear, "Sin *shall not* have dominion over you." There is no reason for you to be any longer a poor helpless victim; you have a *right* to say that "sin shall not have dominion." The Lord has done all He can do on the cross, and He has sent the Holy Spirit to carry out in you all that was done at Calvary for you, so that always at the back of your refusing to let sin reign is the power and energy of the Holy Spirit. You will never wrestle against and conquer sin by your own nature, for *your own nature welcomes it.* Thank God, the least bit of rebellion in you against anything that is wrong in or around you is *from God.*

Welcome the rebellion in you against being in bondage to sin! Surely *that* did not come from the old fallen nature. Yes, rebel against anything in you that is contrary to the redemption in Christ. "But," you say, "there are things which so quickly knock me over." Do not yield to despair. You *rebel* against it, and it is the

Holy Spirit who arouses that rebellion. Do not be passive even toward doubtful things and say, "This must be God's will," or, "I am 'afflicted' with a bad temper." *Go to Romans 6* and read: "Our old man *was* crucified with Him . . . that we should not be in bondage to sin."*

In connection with this, however, you need to keep in mind the difference between the completed work of Christ on the cross and the *experiential working out* of it in you individually—the difference between what Christ has done *"once and for all,"* which you hold by faith, and what has yet to be done in you moment by moment. As you hold the footing of faith—that the "old man" has been crucified—the material the devil works upon in the old creation is *progressively brought into death;* then, on the basis of that death with Christ, the Holy Spirit builds up in you the "new creation."

* There is balance needed here. We must not forget that the Christian life is never to be one of tense self-effort. The activities of physical life—such as breathing—are a self-conscious effort only when the body is sick. When we are healthy our breathing is not labored; nor do we need to remind ourselves continually that we must breathe to live. This is equally true of the spiritual life. So many of us try by mental effort to "reckon ourselves to be dead indeed unto sin, but alive unto God . . . ," and it just does not work. But once this liberty has been shown to us by the Spirit of Life in Christ Jesus (see Romans 8:2), it becomes the simple basis of life to walk in the Spirit. All our complicated intellectual approach is set aside, and stress and strain prevail only when we are sick and out of harmony with the will of God. Spiritual truth is revealed to us by the Holy Spirit in such a way that we may trust and live in the light of the knowledge given to us. This is equally true of all that follows concerning conflict with the powers of evil; and an inbuilt resistance begins to be formed in us to all Satan's works and wiles, while self-conscious effort on our part is stilled.

Briefly, this is how we pass by experience into the "warfare plane." As the spiritual man grows, and is more and more freed by the cross from the old life, he finds he has to take by faith the whole armor of God—which is wholly divine, and is only to be taken and used in the power of the Holy Spirit to wrestle against his spiritual foes.

CHAPTER 4

THE PRAYER BATTLE

"IN the warfare plane, is much time and wrestling necessary?" someone asks. To this we answer: Yes, every minute of your time is necessary—"*praying always* with all prayer and supplication in the spirit." You need to pray over everything, for protection from the foes watching to break in upon your life. This does not mean always on your knees, but a "praying without ceasing" in your spirit.

For this there needs to be a "discernment of spirits" (1 John 4:1). It is only as we advance in spiritual growth that we apprehend that our foes are actually spirit beings, distinct personal entities. They are geographically *in* a place, or they are geographically *out* of it. They come, and they go away when they are defeated (James 4:7). In order to recognize and defeat them you must recognize the reality of their existence. As long as they are vaguely described as an "influence" you will fail to obtain real victory over them; just as when you think of the Holy Spirit only as an "influence" you lose the knowledge of Him as a Person.

"Warfare" prayer is simply saying to God: *"Lord, we are aware of the presence of enemies, but we* DO NOT WANT THEM, *and we have a right to exemption from their presence, because of the victory of Christ at Calvary over Satan and all his hosts."*

Sometimes you cannot discern the cause of pressure. In seeking the cause you may attribute to yourself things which do not belong to you at all, and that may be why you do not get through to victory. You go to Romans 6 and lay hold of it—you pray, you read, you use every weapon you know—but there is no victory. Why? *You are putting your condition down to the wrong cause.* If you were to say: "All this irritation in my nervous system, and the pressure upon my spirit, shows that the enemy is attacking me. I refuse it all in the name of Christ, and claim complete freedom through His precious blood"—you would probably get freedom at once. Romans 6 did not work because the cause of the trouble was not the *old life* but the *enemy.* The Holy Spirit can only bear witness to what is true. If it was the "old Adam life" manifesting itself, and you rested on Romans 6, the Spirit of God would at once bear witness and deliver. But if the trouble comes from an attack of the adversary, and you recognize it and appeal to God for exemption and deliverance on the ground of the finished work of Christ, the Holy Spirit will immediately bear witness to that.

Pray for light, and test the weapons God has given, and when you find the right one, then—it works!

CHAPTER 5

THE PLACE OF THE WILL IN "WARFARE"

"It is God which worketh in you both to will and to do of His good pleasure" (Philippians 2:13).

THIS does not mean that God wills or chooses instead of you, but that God works in you to bring you to the point of exercising the act of choice. It is so with the unsaved. God the Holy Spirit will strive with a sinner to bring him to the point where he himself must *choose,* "wherefore choose life. . . ." It is taking your stand on God's side all the time.

It is helpful to take a position of intelligent choice at every point before entering upon any piece of work for God. When I was in Finland I had a fellow-worker with me, and we used to say together, when we had to decide on various steps: "We choose the will of God in this." By our frequent declaration, we always kept unbiased in everything. Her mind went one way, mine perhaps another, but when we stood together and said *"We choose God's will in this,"* we found ourselves guided into one course and everything went well. It is very important, when two are working together, to keep in the will of God—two "wills" walking as one, because they both choose the will of God.

How the enemy tortures when we think we have *missed the will of God!* Always remember in connection with discerning the will of God that such discernment does not eliminate the need for a childlike trust in God. When by an act of choice you put your will with God's will, you must *trust God* definitely to lead you into the path of His will, though you may not see the way He is leading. Even when God gives you discernment to know His will, there is a limit. You can go too far over "discerning," and cease to have TRUST. The very seeking to discern what is the will of God may bring the mind into a strain, so that you lose quiet trust in Him.

Then there are those who submit to everything around them as God's will because they do not discern the things that differ. Always recognize that God has His will for you, and the devil has a will for you, and you have also your own will. When in doubt about any course, you can say, "I choose the will of God in this," and the Holy Spirit will work along the line of your choice. God, as your Creator, has given you a free will, and He asks for the *voluntary consent* of your will to His. The believer has a right to be free from the workings of evil supernatural powers. You are the one to say "I will not" to Satan, just as you are the one to say "I will" to God. And *God is faithful;* He will bring you through, not *somehow* but *triumphantly!*

CHAPTER 6

"BE FILLED IN SPIRIT"

Ephesians 5:18 ASV, m.

THIS is the marginal reading of a verse much quoted in connection with the emphasizing of the need of the believer's infilling with the Holy Spirit, and generally it is taken to mean that Paul urged the Ephesians to "drink deeply of God's Spirit" (*Weymouth*), or to "be filled with the Spirit," but little is said about the *place* of the Holy Spirit's indwelling, so that much ignorance prevails as to the conditions of the Holy Spirit's "filling," and the way of the believer's co-operation with the Spirit so that He may be able to lead the soul on into spiritual maturity and the knowledge of God.

It is not generally known by ordinary readers of the Bible that in the Greek manuscripts, from which our English text is taken, there are no capital letters employed, and that what we would call a small "s" is used both for the Spirit of God and man's own spirit. Hence, in the margin of Ephesians 5 verse 18, an *alternative* reading is given. The text can mean "Be filled with the Spirit," i.e., with the Spirit of God, or "Be filled *in spirit*," i.e., the *place* which the Holy Spirit fills and indwells.

In contrast with the first part of the verse, the latter reading is very suggestive. The apostle says, "Be not drunken with wine," i.e., which fills the body, but "be filled *in spirit*," i.e., so that your body is dominated and controlled by the law of the Spirit of life in Christ Jesus. "Filled *in spirit*" (not in body), the believer will find utterance *from his spirit* in "psalms and hymns and *spiritual* songs" with an attitude of thankfulness, and easily yield to others when it can be done "in the fear of God."

The spirit of man (i.e., "my spirit," 1 Corinthians 5:3–4; 2:11) is the organism, so to speak, or capacity in man, which is renewed by the new birth (John 3:6; Romans 8:9), and brought into communication with God; and is then capable of being made the residence of the Holy Spirit of God. It is the inner shrine where God dwells, and which can be expanded in capacity for an ever-increasing "filling" of the Holy Spirit. It is by His Spirit in the "inward man," i.e., the regenerate human spirit (*Moule*), that the believer is strengthened to apprehend the vastness of the love of God, and be "filled unto all the fulness of God" (Ephesians 3:16–19, *ASV*).

To be thus "*filled in spirit*" by the Holy Spirit, the spirit of the man must be "divided" from the entanglements of the "soul" (Hebrews 4:12), the work being done by the Word of God "piercing to the joints and marrow," and revealing the mental thoughts and conceptions which come from the soul and do not belong to the spirit. The spirit cannot expand in capacity, and be open to the Spirit of God for specific infillings for special need, unless it is thus liberated from soul bonds. But when it is gradually freed by surrender to the knife work of the Word of God, the believer becomes "strong in spirit" (Luke 1:80); and walking "after the spirit" (Romans 8:4)—note the small "s,"* indicating the spirit of the man, brought into the *ruling position over soul and body*—he learns to *read his spirit,* as Paul did; and by its being "pressed" (Acts 18:5) or "bound" (Acts 20:22), or enlarged with a specific influx of the Holy Spirit for authority over the powers of darkness (Acts 13:9–10), he knows the mind of God, and how to co-operate in spirit with the Holy Spirit.

Prayer warfare against the powers of darkness can only be understood and entered into by those who are "spiritual," i.e., who "walk after the spirit," and not "after the *soul*"; for it is distinctly a *spirit* warfare against *spirit* foes. *Mental* apprehension of the "warfare" is not enough! Real actual "command" over the spirit foes of Christ and His church is only possible "in the *spirit.*" To "be filled in spirit" by the Spirit of God is therefore a necessity for the real apprehension and experiential proving of the truths exemplified in the life of Christ and His apostles in their authority over the powers of darkness (Luke 10:17).

* Editor's note: Evidently the author had access to a version of the Bible with a lower case "s" at this point, likely the *Revised Version* of 1881. Some other translations using a lower case "s" are *The New American Bible* (1970) and Farrar Fenton's translation (1903).

CHAPTER 7

DISCERNING BETWEEN
SOUL AND SPIRIT

Hebrews 4:12

WHEN the spirit is open to God, free and dominant, it becomes God's channel for the Holy Spirit. In the early days of the Christian life the conflict is between spirit and flesh, but when you learn the meaning of the cross and have "crucified the flesh," the "flesh" side of things ceases to *dominate* the life. Then comes a much more subtle conflict—a conflict between spirit and soul; i.e., the *"mental" life seeks to dominate the spirit.* The soul-life—the intellectual and emotional life—is always seeking to get above the spirit, when in God's order the spirit should be ruling and controlling the intellect, emotions, and all that make up the "soul."

Note that the "soul-life" is not to be killed, nor quenched, but is to be *subservient to the spirit.* Your personality—which is practically the "soul" in its human organism—is not to be annihilated. It is the "old

Adam" life which would manifest itself through your personality which is to be taken to the cross (Galatians 5:24), leaving "yourself" as a person to be governed by the Holy Spirit in your spirit, through which God expresses Himself in your life.

COUNTERFEITS OF THE SPIRIT-LIFE

ONE clear, strong principle for meeting all the supernatural manifestations of today is: *One should not accept anything supernatural until he is sure of its source.*

How little many believers understand what is "spirit"—and how many live in the soul (*sensuous*) realm and call it "spirit." There are experiences in the soul-life which *appear* to be spiritual, but are sensuous, and wholly in the realm of the body. When the Lord said that "virtue had gone out of Him" He felt it in His *spirit*, for He lived a true spirit life. He perceived in His *spirit* (Luke 8:46); He rejoiced in *spirit*, He groaned in *spirit*. He felt and knew all things in His spirit.

The counterfeits of today are generally wrought upon the soulish or sense life of believers who have not learned to distinguish between soul and spirit. The church is not only "carnal" (fleshly), but is calling the "soulish" spiritual. The deceiving spirits work upon this ignorance, and only through bitter tears are the eyes of many of God's children being opened to deceptions *in the highest altitudes of the Christian life*, and they are coming to understand the true "life after the spirit" set forth in Paul's epistles.*

Nothing supernatural should be felt by the senses, but by the spirit. Let the Lord's children ask Him to teach them to know what is spirit and what is soul in their inner lives (Hebrews 4:12); then they will understand.

---

* It cannot be too strongly emphasized that there is also a grave danger of the *human spirit* acting apart from the Spirit of God, thus giving ground to the enemy to produce counterfeit spiritual experiences, or counterfeit "guidance." The believer needs to know that *because* he is spiritual his spirit is open to two forces of the spiritual realm—in a way not possible to those who "walk after the flesh," or the carnal life of nature. If he mistakenly believes that only the Holy Spirit can influence him, he is misled, for that would make him *infallible*. He needs to pray for keen discernment. "Prove your own selves" (2 Corinthians 13:5).

CHAPTER 9

THE "SOUL-LIFE" EXPRESSED IN SPEECH

Galatians 5:25

IN prayer, refuse to have a sense of "lack of time." Choose to pray slowly, deliberately, with the force of your spirit in it. There can be the manifestation of the "soul life" in prayer. You may begin to pray in the spirit, and then get down into the "soul" by a rush of words from the up-rising of the natural life.

There is also a "talking" of the natural life that ought to go to the cross—a perpetual outflow of "talk" impossible to follow, for it confuses the mind and *quenches the spirit*. Watch this, and do not put volubility down to your "upbringing" or temperament, for neither of these should check the Holy Spirit. Whatever your temperament may be, you should ask God to make you deliberate in speech. Even in the commonest words, let there be intelligent, deliberate *thought* at the back of them. "Let your speech be *always* with grace" (Colossians 4:6, *ASV*). This will do more for your spiritual life than you can imagine.

Remember, evil spirits can take hold of the tongue and set it going like a talking machine, and if you have much *spiritual knowledge*, which you try to make use of at such times, the consequences are much worse.

CHAPTER 10

KEEPING THE MIND FREE
FOR THE SPIRIT

THERE are laws of the mind which we need to know, e.g., *when it is working easily there is no strain, and as soon as it is strained it ceases its easy working.* The Holy Spirit in your spirit gives light to your mind. When the enemy drives the mind, or it becomes strained or forced in action, it ceases to have the capacity of receiving light from the Holy Spirit. The demoniacal powers know this and do all they can to push you to strain your mind. It can be strained by dwelling on one theme until it cannot see anything else clearly, or by worry, anxiety, or even excessive "thinking" as to what is the will of God. The mind ought to be the channel for light, given through the spirit, by the Spirit of God.

In co-working with others we need to understand that we ought not to break into the trend of the other's thoughts and thus cause strain on the mind. No one can do consecutive thinking, or *spiritual* thinking, if the laws governing the action of the mind under the teaching of the Holy Spirit are broken. In business, if an employer is dealing with some very important matter requiring unbroken action of his mind, his clerk does not come right in upon him and say: "Excuse me, I must ask you so-and-so." But in the Lord's work, the mind of one worker can be easily disturbed and kept from quiet, calm action by the thoughtless dealing of one worker with another. You should not speak to another without attempting to find out before you speak what is the trend of that one's mind at the moment. In helping souls, too, you should first find out the point they are at *mentally*, meet them there, and then lead them right on, *spiritually*, to intelligently apprehended truth.

There are many who are suffering from over-strain; not from real work, mental or spiritual, but from the ignorant breaking of God's laws for the mind.

Moreover, when you are working with another and you do not see "eye to eye" mentally, you can still be of *one spirit* if you walk after the spirit. Understand this and you will delight in discovering all the different points of view God gives His children. God is the only One with an infinite mind. If you remember that you have only a *finite* mind, you will not want everyone to see eye to eye with you in everything.

CHAPTER 11

VICTORY IN CONFLICT

IT does not matter how "spiritual" you are—how fully God dwells in your spirit, or how carefully you "walk after the spirit"—you still have to meet a spirit foe, and the attacks of that foe are mainly *against the spirit* in the spiritual man. At one stage of the Christian life the attack may be on the mind, driving it into over-activity or dullness; or on the body in various ways; but the truly spiritual believer will find phases of conflict unknown in the earlier stages of the Christian life.

When you come into circumstances which the powers of darkness are using to attack you, the danger is to be not on guard concerning the effect this is having *on your spirit*. There may be a sense of disappointment, opposition, pain, or bondage, coming into the spirit. You are "down," "pressed," and disturbed because the *spirit* is being attacked, through the enemy using circumstances or people against you. At such a time the first thing to do is not to oppose anything in the people, or in the atmosphere, but to *keep your spirit untouched and free,* holding your union with Christ, abiding in Him by faith; secondly, *refuse* the attack of the enemy on your spirit, and then *claim the full victory of the cross* over all the powers of darkness in the atmosphere around you. Learn to be still and calm *in God.* Hold the victory of faith, and you will come out victoriously.

Your spirit will not be fully at the disposal of God if it is crushed, bound, or in personal conflict. You must have a free spirit; therefore take care to get it free and keep it so. Then as you are disengaged in spirit, God will find in you a right instrument for His work. Many are out of tune with God because they are not up to date in prayer, and in obedience to the Holy Spirit, and in all that keeps the spirit free for God. We must recognize the need of getting the "emotions" of the soul stilled so as to watch for the Spirit-leading of God—what men of God in centuries past used to mean when they spoke of "quietness of soul." Why this need? *To get the soul-life still* so that the spirit can ascend and rule.

CHAPTER 12

THE "LAW OF PASSIVITY"

"I also labour, striving according to His working, which worketh in me mightily" (Colossians 1:29).

THIS is only one of the scriptures which clearly show the necessity for the full active use of the whole outer man in God's service. God works mightily—I work mightily. That is absolutely contrary to the idea many have that God works through a man like water goes through a pipe—simply passes power through him while he remains passive!

As Christians, we perhaps know little of spiritists, probably have never read their books or come in contact with them, and it is not always recognized that those who practice spiritism do really have communication with spirits—evil *spirits*. Although there are failures and deceptions and even quackery in spiritism, these only serve to cover up the real work of Satan. You will find, however, that the one condition and principle which mediums have to fulfill in order to obtain spirit communication and working is this: Every part of the whole being must be perfectly passive and out of action. The brain must be blank, the faculties dormant, the will "let go," and the body passive. *This absolute passivity is the fundamental law for the working of evil spirits through human beings.* A minister told me of a girl medium whom he visited with. He asked her how she became one, and she replied that she "sat in a dark room once a day, and *gave herself up* to the spirits." *They* say they are good spirits, but the fact is, there are no good spirits with whom you can obtain any communication.

By dismissing these things as "nothing" we have missed understanding the *law* by which these evil spirits work, the "law of passivity." There is not one sentence in Paul's epistles where he tells you to become "passive." Every time he speaks of the Holy Spirit there is a reference to activity on the part of the believer. "*I labour,* striving according to His working." God works "according to law," and the law for the working of the Holy Spirit is "active co-operation." The law for the working of evil spirits is passive submission. God desires "fellow workers with Him": evil spirits want to *use you* as a passive instrument.

Q. What about yielding ourselves to God?

A. You will not find a single place in the Bible where the command or principle is laid down that your faculties are to be out of use. The Apostle Paul speaks of spiritual understanding: "The eyes of your understanding being enlightened." Nor are you ever told in

God's Word that your will is to be passive. You are constantly enjoined to have an active will—"put on"—"put off"—"lay hold"—"fight"! If, then, passivity is the law for evil supernatural powers to work, and you as a believer (*knowingly or unknowingly*) fulfill that law in any degree, *they will work.*

Passivity will account for much disappointment in the spiritual life. For instance, you wanted to be guided by God, and you thought He would tell you, supernaturally, what to do; but He did not, and you were disappointed, or thought you had sinned in some way. God has not done many things you asked or expected, because you failed to fulfill the law by which He has chosen to work. He manifests His power by working in and *through you,* not *instead of you!* Many have supposed that if believers have power from God He will work without their co-operation, and consequently have dropped into a state of passivity, and that is the explanation for so much deception, on the one hand, and powerlessness, on the other.

One section of the church is deceived with supernatural workings, and the other is powerless and inactive in God's service. God does not break His own law of cause and effect. If you touch a "live" wire, you will get an electric shock! As a believer, you must walk according to God's laws, then He will guard you. But there is a "law of passivity" which, if obeyed, enables evil spirits to work; and if children of God will persist in expecting God to move their bodies without their own volition, they fulfill that law; and all their devotion and claiming the protection of the blood of Christ will not save them from spiritist manifestations as they fulfill the law for producing them.

What is true surrender to God? You surrender *sin*, by dropping it; you surrender *yourself*, by giving up your whole being to be available in His service. "Yield yourselves unto God as those that are alive from the dead" (Romans 6:13). Not as a machine or an automaton. Actively obey God. You presented your members to sin once; now present them to God. Stand for Him, actively and fully, with every part of your being. "To whom ye yield yourselves . . . his servants ye are" (Romans 6:16). *Servants* of God! What is a servant for, but to serve? Of what use is a passive servant?

"I plead with you . . . *present all your faculties* to Him as a living and holy sacrifice acceptable to Him" (Romans 12:1, *Weymouth*).

Q. How do you distinguish between the mind being passive and the mind being "silent" to God?

A. The mind being "passive" means that it is sluggish and heavy, and unable to act and think; while the mind being "silent unto God" is simply an awakened, liberated mind refraining from healthy action in other directions, so as to be quiet before the Lord! The mind should, in its normal condition, be awake, but not full of rushing, uncontrollable thoughts. It should be always keenly alert to see the mind of the Spirit at the moment, by being awake to every duty and to everything in your environment—able to see, to watch, to catch, to think; ready to act as God gives you light, and moves in your spirit to the doing of His will. Briefly, if the mind is purely "quiet" it is ready for action at any moment. When the mind is passive it is NOT FREE TO ACT.

There is both a right and a wrong quietness. The first is best described as pliability to every indication of the will of God, so that, with ease, the believer turns, moment by moment, as directed by the Holy Spirit. The second—a wrong "quietness," or *passivity*—is allowing the mental and other faculties to lie dormant, which makes the man as one *acted upon* by an unseen power, rather than one energized by the Holy Spirit intelligently to work with God. This comes about through having a mistaken idea of what being "channels only" or "instruments used by God" means, and this again is often the swinging to another extreme in fear of the activity of the "flesh." The believer desiring to be "spiritual" sees clearly how the natural intellect and reason hinders the apprehension of the things of the Spirit, and so he imagines that the intellect must not be called into use, and some even take a pride in saying that they have "not been to college," and have had no "teaching of man" at all.

All this swinging to extremes comes through the lack of teaching concerning the inner meaning of the cross, and the deeper knowledge of the cross which should come to the believer really progressing in the spiritual life. The common idea that the Christian is "done with the cross" when he is justified by faith and has apprehended his judicial death with Christ prevents the Holy Spirit from leading the soul into Philippians

3:10 and 2 Corinthians 4:10–12 in their deepest meaning. In other words, the Christian assumes that he has entered a position through his justification—namely judicial "death"—where he only needs to draw upon the *life* of Christ—forgetting that the negative, or fellowship with the *death* of Christ, is the necessary *complement* of the positive inflow of the risen life of the Lord. Consequently, he expects the Lord to add the "new" to the "old" without his progressively yielding the "old" to death to make room for the "new" (Romans 8:13).

What has this to do with wrong passivity? This: that the intellectual powers need to be brought under the death-work of the cross, so that the *natural* activity of the mind may cease. It is this soulish activity of mind which the spiritual man fears, but *the remedy is not passivity*—or refusing to use the mind—but the *renewing* of the mind through the death-power of the cross so that the "mind of Christ" becomes increasingly wrought into the believer, and he receives a "sound mind," usable by the Holy Spirit to its fullest capacity. Then the reasoning powers will become more acute and alert than in the time of their soulish activity; and wisdom from above will take the place of the natural wisdom. See James 1:5; 3:17.

The outcome of wrong passivity is two-fold: (1) a lack of intellectual power through the habit of not using the mind, whereas the mental capacity of every child of God should reach its fullest development through the renewing of the Spirit; (2) all passivity of mind gives ground to *evil* powers to work upon the man, and to use him unknown to himself, for the Holy Spirit does not so much work *upon* as work *with* the believer, i.e., He seeks the whole man as a fully developed and intelligent co-worker, not merely a passive machine. The believer *is* an "instrument," but not one passively wielded so much as intelligently energized, with every faculty awake and usable. Colossians 1:29 most concisely shows this, and Philippians 3:13. "I labour" means *toil*, and "stretching forward" speaks of every nerve and muscle—spiritual, mental and physical—at full bent in pressing on in the life of God.

You ask if Satan can make an impression when the mind is "silent before God." Yes, if you allow the "silence" to drop into passivity, or inertness. You must learn to recognize how he makes impressions: first, by suggestions to the mind—thus indirectly influencing the spirit; second, by pressure on your spirit—thus indirectly influencing your mind.

CHAPTER 13

CONTROL OF THE IMAGINATION

O NE of Satan's greatest strongholds lies in the *imagination*. Some of you have suffered from your "vivid imagination" from childhood, and it is a marvelous gospel that brings you light as to how you may be set free from an inflamed imagination. Perhaps you have daydreams—your mind carries you away against your will; or mental pictures—awful pictures of things that are going to happen—until you can scarcely endure it; or you once saw something dreadful happen, and for the rest of your life you are haunted by it. You have asked God to take it away. You have shut your mind, closed your eyes, refused to look—but with no relief. Then the enemy has told you lies about it— said you were "born with a vivid imagination" or that it is "natural." But *it can all be stopped* and lifelong suffering ended by recognizing that it is an evil spirit flashing these pictures into the imagination.

Then there are "pictures" of other people. Has it ever occurred to you why you should imagine such and such a person is "jealous" of you? You meet your friend, and you say: "She did not look kindly at me; there is something wrong, I am sure"—and probably there was not a trace of it in reality! This is the cause of divisions and endless waste of time among God's children. You see a band of God's people, every heart and will seemingly surrendered to Him, but the powers of darkness are playing with their imaginations, and setting one against another, until there is nothing but friction. Yet many of them are *afraid of the light that would put a stop to it all!* Surrender to God does not bring absolute liberation of the mind and body at one stroke! Liberation comes up to the point where you have knowledge to reject what is not of God! *Recognize, refuse,* and then *ignore,* the "pictures" given to your imagination by the enemy. You try to conquer, but *fail*—until at last you discover and own that the enemy holds your imagination. Then you say: "Calvary is victory over all the power of the enemy. I claim absolute exemption on the ground of the precious blood of Christ from all of Satan's interference with my mind or imagination." Then carry out your declaration by refusing all ground you have ever given in mind or imagination: refuse the thoughts as they come, and then ignore them. Do not dwell upon them. "Ye shall *know the truth*, and the truth shall make you free." What right has the enemy to interfere with a child of God? None whatever! The moment he is recognized, and refused in the name of Jesus, he is bound to flee.

Perhaps you have been thinking it was "yourself" all the time, and the devil has been beating you for what he himself was doing. Are you willing to say: "It was not *me*, it was against my will. *I do not consent* to these imaginations! It was an evil spirit of Satan suggesting things to my mind, and I refuse it all in the name of the Lord Jesus Christ who conquered him at Calvary"? I agree that this truth is not palatable, but it is folly to remain in bondage because you will not call things by their right names! Claim exemption from the power of the enemy in spirit, soul and body. You have as much right to that as to victory over sin.

The power of the Holy Spirit in your spirit is the power to drive these things out, but you must needs recognize them, and set your will against them. It is the Lord who does the work, but *you* have to set the helm right. That is the way they manage a ship! The man at the helm puts the helm right, and the engine-power makes the ship go. Do you believe that you can have your imagination liberated, your memory under control, and all the faculties of the mind free so that, "the eyes of your understanding being filled with light," you may be able to use the weapons of your warfare to the pulling down of the devil's strongholds, "casting down imaginations, and every high thing that exalteth itself against the knowledge of God, and bringing into captivity every thought to the obedience of Christ" (2 Corinthians 10:4–5)? Then you will have no inflamed ideas about others in your mind, and your spirit will be liberated, and your body, instead of dominating you, will be brought under control and set free to carry out God's will. This is the path of victory, practical and real!

Q. Can we be so garrisoned, within as well as without, that suggestions from the enemy can be clearly recognized?

A. I would say "Yes," for when your mind is brought into clear light, and your spirit into union with the Lord Jesus Christ, the blessed Spirit of God will make you, as you mature, intuitively recognize thoughts suggested by the enemy, however beautifully they are clothed. Sometimes you may discern a thing to be from the adversary, though you cannot say why to others, for your recognition comes simply from your union with the Lord Jesus Christ. When your spirit is in true, pure union with Christ, you will often find that things said by others to be "of God" are met by "deadness" in your spirit; and you must never go against that restraint in your spirit. We need to know this spiritual fact now, when the enemy is counterfeiting the things of God so terribly, for there is not a single truth of God that Satan is not imitating. *The enemy pushes truth too far, so that it becomes error;* and even what is true can absorb you too much, so that you become blind to all else. Whenever one thing possesses your mind so that you *cannot think of anything else,* it has gone too far, because if one truth occupies your mind entirely, it closes it to God's fresh revelations; and this is not a healthy spiritual condition.

Q. How can you guarantee that you are obeying God, and God only? Is it possible for a Christian to be led or guided by evil spirits?

A. Nobody can *guarantee* that he or she is obeying God, and "God only," IN SUPERNATURAL guidance, because there are so many factors liable to intervene, i.e., one's own mind, his own spirit, his own will, and the possibility of the intrusion of deceiving spirits.

Evil spirits can counterfeit God as Father, Son or Holy Spirit, and the believer needs to know very clearly the principles upon which God works, so as to detect between the divine and the satanic.

There is also a "discerning of spirits" which is a spiritual gift, but this requires knowledge of "doctrine" (1 John 4:1), so as to understand doctrine which is of God and doctrines or teachings from teaching spirits.

There is, then, the simple detecting, at a glance, of which spirit is at work—the true or the false; and also a test of spirits which has to do with *doctrinal* matters. In the former situation a believer can tell by knowledge in his spirit that lying spirits are at work in a meeting or in a person, but he may not have the understanding needed for *testing the "doctrines"* of the spirits set forth by the teacher. He needs knowledge in both cases: knowledge to read his spirit with assurance, in the face of all the surface appearances that the supernatural workings are "of God," and knowledge to detect the subtlety of "teachings" bearing certain indications of emanating from the pit, yet appearing to be from God.

Remember, there is a difference between *false* teachers and *deceived* ones. There are many deceived ones among devoted teachers today, because they do not recognize that an army of teaching spirits have come forth from the abyss to deceive the people of

God, and that the special peril of the spiritual section of the church lies in the supernatural realm, whence the deceiving spirits with *"teachings"* are whispering their lies to all who are "spiritual," i.e., open to spiritual things. The "teaching spirits" with "doctrines" will make special efforts to deceive those who have to transmit "doctrine," and seek to mingle *their* teachings with *truth,* so as to get them accepted. Every believer must test all "teachers" for himself by the Word of God and by *their attitude to the atonement,* and not be misled into testing teachings by the character of the man. Good men can be deceived, and Satan needs good men to float his lies under the guise of truth.

The fact that "honest souls" can be deceived is sufficiently clear in the case of Eve, and the warning based thereon in 2 Corinthians 11:3. Eve was ignorant of the devices of the watching enemy. To be true in motive, and faithful up to light, is not sufficient safeguard against deception. It is not safe to rely upon sincerity in oneself as a safeguard, any more than reliance upon self in any other way. To "prove all things" is necessary, recognizing our ignorance and the need of light from God to unveil the enemy. See 1 Thessalonians 5:21 and 1 John 4:1.

The PRIMARY TEST OF THE WORD OF GOD must be applied to all "teachings." *Not isolated texts from the Word, nor portions of the Word.* Remember also, Satan may back up false teaching by "signs and wonders" (Matthew 24:24; 2 Thessalonians 2:9; Revelation 13:13), so "fire from heaven," obvious "power" and "signs," are not proof of any teaching being of God;

nor is a beautiful life, for Satan's "ministers" can be "ministers of righteousness" (2 Corinthians 11:13–15). The test is "doctrine" (1 John 4:2–3), tested by the truth revealed in the Scriptures.

In the matter of *personal* obedience to God, however, the believer can detect whether he is obeying God in some "command" by judging its fruits (i.e., God has always a purpose in His commands) and by knowledge of the character of God, i.e., that He will give no command to action out of harmony with His character and Word.

Q. How do you define true guidance, or "leading"?

A. Many define guidance, or "leading," as purely and only supernatural, such as by a voice saying "Do this" or "Do that," or by a compulsory movement or impulse, apart from the action or volition of the believer himself, thinking of the expression used of the Lord, "the Spirit driveth Him into the wilderness" (Mark 1:12). But this was abnormal in the life of Christ, and implies intense spirit conflict wherein the Holy Spirit overmastered the ordinary and normal actions of His being. We have a glimpse into a similar intense movement of His spirit in John 11:38, when, "groaning with indignation in His spirit," He moved to the grave of Lazarus. In both instances He was moved forward to direct conflict with Satan—in the case of Lazarus, with Satan as the Prince of Death. The Gethsemane agony was of the same nature.

But normally Christ was guided, or led, in simple

fellowship with the Father: deciding, acting, reasoning, thinking, as one who knew the will of God and intelligently (I speak reverently) carried it out. The "voice" from heaven was rare and, as the Lord Himself said, was for the sake of others, not Himself. He knew the Father's will and, with every faculty of His being as Man, did it.

As Christ was a pattern or example for His followers, this shows guidance, or "leading," in its perfect and true form, and believers can expect the co-working of the Holy Spirit only when they walk after the pattern of their Example. Out of line with the Pattern, they cease to have the working of the Holy Spirit and become open to the deceptive counterfeit workings of the powers of darkness.

If the believer ceases to use mind, reason, will, and all his other faculties as a "person" and depends upon voices or impulses for guidance, he will be "led" or guided by evil spirits feigning to be God.

Q. How can I have the cross so working in my life that my family SEE IT, and are brought into the light of God? I am in business, and get so tried at times. Sometimes I think I am "put upon" and I speak sharply—I may not get into a temper, but it is inside!

A. First of all you need to know how to put Romans 6 into practice in your daily business life. For this it is necessary to understand how to live in your *will*. The moment you *choose* God's will, the power of God is at the back of your choice to bring it into effect. You must therefore live by your choice, and not by your feelings. At the beginning of the day, deliberately assert your choice and will—that all through this day your position is "crucified with Christ." This is the basic position of faith. God says that in Christ "you died," and you stand on that fact and reckon it true.

The attitude of "death" is the negative side, the side of separation from sin and Satan; but the positive, conquering side of the Calvary message is the "life of Jesus" in you—"GREATER IS HE THAT IS IN YOU than he that is in the world" (1 John 4:4). As you deliberately take the attitude that you have been crucified with Christ, and reckon yourself "dead to sin" *now,* so you also reckon upon the life of Jesus, imparted to you by the Holy Spirit, that Christ may now be your strength and power. That is your attitude, your choice, your will, in the morning.

Now comes the conflict with the wicked spirits of Satan as they seek to drive the believer from this position. Outside of your personal volition and position there are hosts of wicked spirits, instructed by Satan to watch you. He has said to them: "That person has taken her position at the cross, and chosen the position of death to sin; she has determined that today Christ shall have the victory in her life. Now watch her, stir up those around her to attack her, shoot at her, put upon her—and if you keep on long enough you will bring her down from that position!"

But the foolish thing is, we blame "people" for what the enemy is doing. If you recognize that it is Satan at the back of it all, you will refuse to be upset by whatever happens. This is an aspect of the overcoming life that many of God's children have failed to see. They have been occupied thinking how *they* can get victory, and have not recognized that *the powers of darkness* were heaping fuel on the fire or attacking them through others. While the "world rulers" have been attacking, the believer has thought the trouble came from "self," instead of holding the victory and resisting the true cause at the back of "flesh and blood." The poor soul is struggling to conquer "self" when the onslaught is really from the powers of darkness.

Take, for instance, the statement just made: "They *put upon* me." Why not say instead: "It is the enemy pushing them to 'put upon' me. Lord, I trust Thee to stop him"? The true way of victory does not *always* lie in receiving power to "bear" the imposition of others. Very often there is need of insight into the *cause* at the back of it, and prayer to God to deal with the cause.

"You must *bear* this—it is your cross!" How the deceiver can get behind the very truth of God and use it to crush you! It may not be God who puts that "cross" upon you, but the enemy, and you must not passively endure suffering which comes from the devil. The cross God asks you to bear is not necessarily "trial," but fellowship with the Lord Jesus in the *death* aspect of His cross. His cross where He died is your cross, upon which you died and die daily. The "cross" of the devil is not a true cross but his oppression of you, which he wants you to accept as from God.

If you want to know Romans 6 for victory in your daily life, you must know it as an *inside* position, which the enemy will seek by every means to rob you of. You should ask God to reveal to you the enemy's devices, so that when he takes hold of someone's mouth to attack you, you recognize it as the enemy's work and immediately refuse to be affected by it.

Suppose one of your children is cross and unmanageable, and you are perplexed as to what to do. Go to God and ask Him to stop the enemy working upon that child. A lady once told me that every time she went aside to pray, her little boy went into the hall and made such a noise that she had to go to him. At last one day she said: "I believe it is the enemy working on that child to prevent my praying, and I will not go down the next time he does it." The next time she went to prayer, the boy began again; but his mother said: "Lord, if this is the devil at work to hinder me praying, please stop him"—and the little lad stopped his noise at once.

The reason why the position of Romans 6 seems to be of no avail for victory with many souls is that they have failed to recognize the workings of the enemy, and therefore failed to throw him off. "*Greater is He that is in you* than he that is in the world." The manifestation of the "life of Jesus" in you is not just in the Lamb spirit, in sweetness and submissiveness— which must be manifested to the *human* instrument of your testing; there must also be the "Lion spirit" toward the powers of darkness, for this means victory over Satan. The life of Jesus manifested in your mortal body is only *one aspect* of the Christ-life; but "greater is He that is in you than he that is in the world" is another aspect, speaking of victory over Satan and his wicked spirits. It is the power of the *conquering Christ* in us, triumphing over all the attacks of the enemy in the world around. The enemy seeks to drive you in upon yourself. The secret of the overcoming life is to overcome also that which comes upon you from the enemy without.

You can stop the devil, in the name of Jesus. That is the great fact you need to understand. Your victory in Christ is to include not only death to sin for victory over yourself, but the victory of Christ on the cross is also for you to wield over Satan. Even as Christ controlled and commanded the wicked spirits He met with in His earthly career, the same Christ *in you* will do the same, for you are joined to Him in His risen life. But remember that command cannot be exercised unless you recognize the presence and workings of the powers of evil. They trick the people of God by hiding themselves under many names. Ask God to open your eyes, that you may discern the spirits and where they are at work.

CHAPTER 14

WHAT DO WE MEAN BY "STANDING" ON CALVARY?

WE stand on Calvary ground because it is the place where Christ redeemed us from the world, the flesh and the devil, and we stand there as our *faith position*. Take your stand upon the finished work of Christ, and claim His victory; there and there only may you dare to say to the prince of this world, "Go!" When did Christ say it? In the wilderness: "Get thee hence, Satan." Dare you say it? Not in your own name. You dare say it only as you are united to Christ and His life is manifested in you. You stand on Calvary as the ground because it is the place where the old Adam was nailed to the cross, where the question of sin was settled, where the Lord Jesus Christ—God manifest in the flesh—gave His atoning sacrifice for the sins of the whole world. You need constantly to *recognize your position* which has been revealed to you by the Holy Spirit, and to stand on the finished work of Christ.

It is an attitude—*a place from whence you act.* Take

your stand at Calvary where Christ redeemed us, and won the victory over the prince of this world. You have to take that position in everything you do—with regard to sin, to this world, to the enemy, and to everything that is contrary to God. You say: "I stand on redemption ground; I stand at the cross. That is my place and position." Then you dare to say to Satan: *"Go, in Jesus' name,"* for you are joined to his Master and his Conquerer.

Q. What did Paul mean by "That Christ may dwell in your hearts by faith"?

A. I assume no one reading this will say that the Lord Jesus Christ, as the glorified Man in heaven, is dwelling in the believer. Christ in heaven is the very Man that went up in His glorified human body to the throne; and *that* Christ, with the glorified human body, is seated at God's right hand, and is not in anybody's heart, and cannot be. It is Christ *by His Spirit*—"the Spirit of Jesus"—who is in us. "That Christ may dwell in your hearts by faith" means the Lord enthroned in your affections, *by His Spirit.*

Your reliance should never be upon *a Christ within,* but upon *a Christ on the throne in heaven,* who by His Spirit will energize you for all He wants you to do. Your faith is to rest upon the glorified Man in heaven, and as you look to Him there *His Spirit* is poured into your spirit, making Him a reality to you. Paul says, "I trust by the Spirit of Jesus" that I shall do this or that. In the Acts of the Apostles, Luke says, "The Spirit of Jesus suffered them not." So it is the *Spirit* of Jesus who dwells in us.

It is very important that you do not rely upon an inward, subjective experience, but upon God and Christ in the glory. *The reliance upon an inward experience opens the door to Satan's counterfeits.* The faith of the church is to be centered upon Christ on the *throne,* even as He is set forth in the Word. The apostles preached a glorified Christ in *heaven.*

In union with Christ we become "partakers of the divine nature" (2 Peter 1:4), and have the very life of Jesus imparted to us. God revealed His Son—the very nature of His Son—in Paul, but Paul always proclaimed and relied upon the Man Christ Jesus *in heaven,* not upon His nature or His Spirit in himself. To understand this distinction is a great safeguard against Satan's counterfeits. Occupied with Christ as a person on the throne in heaven, your spirit is drawn outward from introspection, self-absorption, self-indulgence— spiritual as well as soulish—and is freed from self-centeredness, to live *out* of yourself, *for* Christ and *in* Christ.

As you thus live out of yourself, all the power of the life of Christ is communicated to you by His Spirit. Notice the Lord's words in John 14:20: At that day ye shall know that (1) "I am in My Father"—Christ in heaven, and (2) "ye in Me"—in heaven, spiritually, and (3) "I in you"—by My Spirit manifested in you. That is quite different to your being occupied entirely with some inward experience. "*Abide in Me*, and *I in you.*" Always the "I in you" follows the "ye in Me"; your spirit in Me—and as the result of being "in Me" I am in you, and My words are in you, and out of you shall flow rivers of living water.

One of the most subtle things the enemy ever did was when he turned the children of God in upon themselves, to seek AN INWARD EXPERIENCE of the baptism of the Holy Spirit, after the Welsh Revival. The advancing ranks of the church were pressing on with a glorious shout of victory when this subtle onslaught came from the enemy and checked it.

I have spoken to you about the fullness of the Holy Spirit, but it will be a very sad thing if it turns you in upon yourselves, watching for an inward experience. Will you, please, with simple choice of will, ask God to remove from within you every obstacle to the mighty influx of His Spirit . . . and then forget yourself and go forward into your work with a persistent giving out of all you know. God will not give you *more* until you have used what you already *have*.

Q. "This is the victory that overcometh . . . even OUR FAITH." Is it not possible to pray, and yet not have faith? I feel I need much more faith—like Jesus commanded: "Have faith in God."

A. The words quoted, "Have faith in God," are really, as shown in the margin, *"Have the faith of God"* (Mark 11:22), and it is well to remember the circumstances in which they were spoken. Jesus was speaking of the barren fig tree. Looking for fruit, He had found nothing upon it but leaves, and He said: "Let no man eat fruit of thee hereafter for ever." The next day they found the tree withered away. Then He turned to the disciples and said: "If you have faith, you shall not only do what I have done to the fig tree, but you shall say to the mountain, 'Be thou removed,' and it shall be done."

The "faith of God" is this, that when *He* speaks the word the thing is *done*. God said, "Let there be light," and there was light. The words you speak are of the greatest importance in the prayer life. In this spiritual sphere, what *you say* creates. To put it more plainly, if you say "I cannot," then you cannot; but if you say "*I can*, through *Christ* who strengthens me," then you *can*. "The faith of God" is the faith which God had when He said: "Let there be light." God does not doubt that it will be as He has said. Think of the words of Christ in this connection: "Have the faith of God"—"If ye have faith . . . ye shall not only do this which is done to the fig tree . . . " (Matthew 21:21). What had He done to the fig tree? He only *spoke* to it, and it withered away. St. Mark's account goes on: " . . . and shall not doubt in his heart, but shall believe that those things *which he saith* shall come to pass; he shall have *whatsoever he saith*."

Remember that your *words* are of importance in the spiritual realm. "They overcame him by the blood of the Lamb, and by *the word of their testimony*." When you come face to face with a difficulty, you may look at it from the human standpoint and say: "I cannot"; but look at it from God's standpoint, and say: "Is it the will of God? If so, *I can! I can do all things through Christ!*" Apply this to everything in your life, and it will make you beware of your words. I say to someone: "You know that is not right," and it almost breaks my heart to hear in reply: "I cannot help it!" I beg you not to say such things, for if you *say* you cannot help it, about something that is wrong, the enemy will come down upon you, and you will *not be able to help it*. Say: "I *can* help it, in the name of *Christ*" (Philippians 4:13).

"Have the faith of God!" How can we put this faith into words, so that what we say *in the will of God* will come to pass? Not by some great charismatic experience, or by some mysterious process, but by beginning to live it out in little things—little matters concerning traveling, or rising, for instance—and the faith will grow as you prove it for yourself. I used to say: "I cannot take a long journey and then go straight into a meeting. I need a rest first." But when, after traveling all day, the Lord made it clear to me to go straight to a meeting and speak, I said: "Of course I can, if that is Thy will"—then the power and strength were given, because I went in the faith that it was the will of God, and that therefore I *could* do it. Then I began to apply this principle to a thousand little things I had thought I could not do. What has this to do with the prayer life? Everything, because unless you triumph in the smaller kingdom of your own life, you will never triumph in the kingdom of Jesus Christ.

Q. How can a consecrated Christian become a successful intercessor with Christ? What is the secret of the blessed art?

A. Much has been written on this subject, which is too great to deal with briefly. The true way of intercession is not intercession *with* Christ, but joined *to*

Christ—one spirit—asking the Father, as in union with Christ; i.e., in His name—*in Him.* Not the attitude of two—i.e., Christ and I—but *one*—union with Christ—asking what He asks—because joined to Him in one life. The *secret* of power in prayer lies in the apprehension of this *union,* so that we are in the right *attitude* and right *place* to pray. Because *union with Christ* is the secret of prayer we find it so linked in John 15:7. As we abide in Christ, He, by His word, abides in us—then "ask what ye will," for you only ask *His* will!

Q. How long are we to continue asking for the same thing?

A. This is a point where we need light in prayer. The Bible says, "Use not vain repetitions," and you need to know whether a thing is in the will of God before you come to a definite transaction with Him about it. One thing you need never be in any doubt about, and that is this clear statement of the Word: "The Son of God was manifested that He might destroy the works of the devil" (1 John 3:8). There is no doubt about the will of God there, and it will cover a great deal of praying. You may be certain you are in the will of God in asking Him to destroy the works of the devil.

Take an illustration. You may say: "Lord, the devil is at work through that man. We ask You to destroy his work there." Are you to keep on with that petition? No! You are, however, to follow up that general prayer by prayer *in detail.* You need to watch and pray all around that man. His circumstances hinder his deliverance—"Lord, deal with his circumstances, and put them right!"

His associates, the places he goes to, everything you see to be an obstacle to his deliverance, deal with in prayer until it is removed. Then you begin to pray for positive blessing, and finally you pray him right through.

You do not know what hinders blessing in a certain church, but you sense there is hindrance to the work of God. Bring it before the Lord, and ask that wherever the enemy is at work he may be *exposed;* that whatever the hindrances are they may be *made manifest.* You will find that definite material for prayer will come to your knowledge until you have prayed it through in every detail, and the work of God is unhindered.

How long are you to pray for the conversion of someone you are interested in? Pray once: "Lord, save my son." The Lord has heard you! Now watch, and pray in detail for everything about him: where he goes, what he reads, his friends, his work—follow it all in prayer. Pray for the same persons, but pray *new prayers!* Do not pray every day, "Lord, save that soul!" but pray around his life and circumstances. *Learn to shepherd souls by prayer*—then you will look at them with different eyes, and God will show you what the hindrances are to their being saved. This will put a stop to gossip! Someone says: "Is it not dreadful about So-and-so?" Once you would have said, "How sad," and passed it on to another; but now you just say: "I thank Thee, Lord, for letting me know this— now I can pray better for that one." So everything you hear is turned into prayer.

Praying is *work.* Pray *out* the obstacles, pray *in* the

positive power, and that will give you abundant material for this work of prayer.

Q. I see that this praying in detail rests in the faith of God—it is not a burdensome duty, but a work of faith.

A. Yes, this is not carrying burdens: it is an attitude of prayer. It means that you ask the Lord to train your mind to be always "watching unto prayer," and the reflex blessing will come upon you. Prayer will burst out of you; you will not be able to look upon a thing without praying over it. This is what God means by "Pray without ceasing."

What a tremendous effect God's people would have upon the world if they went about praying like this. They would be a block in the devil's path by their very presence in a place. You would not see a man's name in the newspaper without praying for him. What would not this mean to our public men?

Q. How far may we, who know something of the liberating power of the cross, claim the deliverance for others?

A. This question opens out a subject of vital importance to the church of God. Some shrink from acknowledging that it is possible for an evil spirit to deceive a true child of God, and yet many have been delivered from the bondage of years through simply recognizing this truth. "When the strong man armed keepeth his palace, his goods are in peace." The "armour" wherein Satan "trusteth" (Luke 11:22) is the *fallen Adam*, and therefore the only position which will despoil the strong man, and take away the ground he holds, is the standing upon Romans 6:6 as a continual basis, i.e., "Our old man *was* crucified with Him." And this, not merely as a past experience or recognized fact, but for every moment, by faith.

This is the reason why Satan so bitterly resists the preaching of the cross, especially in the aspects of Romans 6 and Colossians 2:15, as a fact to be believed and used; for only the believers who stand in steady faith upon Romans 6:11 can prove Colossians 2:15 on behalf of others. Only then, also, can Luke 10:19 become experientially true: "I have given you authority . . . over *all* the power of the enemy." The whole ground and pledge of this is *the finished work of Christ* on the cross, where John 12:31 was fulfilled (see John 16:11); and the only condition for its exercise by the believer is *union with the Conqueror,* as foreshadowed in Luke 10:17.

There are various ways of exercising this authority of Christ over the enemy for others. The believer, standing on the basis of Romans 6:11, reckoning himself in that place where alone he is out of reach of the enemy, may, in the name of Christ, command the evil spirit to depart (Luke 10:17); or, in private prayer, be claiming the efficacy of the finished work of Christ over the enemy, as he grips that soul. The only way in which any believer can enter into this work in practical experience is that given in John 14:26 and John 16:13.

Q. I suppose this would be putting into practice the command to "resist the devil"—"whom resist stedfast in the faith"?

A. Yes, the same basic principle is needed for all our "wrestling" against the powers of evil. Our death with Christ and risen life in Him *alone* puts us in the place of safety. This is the one impregnable rock-position upon which every believer *must* STAND in resisting the powers of darkness. *To look at Romans 6 as only a past experience is a fatal mistake,* and is no safeguard against deception. Many who have done this, looking upon identification with Christ in death as a stage through which they pass to a life on the resurrection side of the cross, have found themselves caught in the most subtle snares of the angel of light, for they were lulled into false security, thinking that they were "dead" and therefore could not be deceived by the Deceiver . . . until he went too far and their eyes were opened to see that the *position* of death is but the basis for a *progressive conformity to death,* which must be brought about in every believer. A moment-by-moment faith—a stedfast *standing* on the fact in the present tense of NOW, i.e., the believer reckoning himself to be dead to sin in the present moment on the basis of identification with Christ in His death—is the strong position for victory over sin and Satan. Standing on the bedrock ground of Romans 6, the believer wields the weapon of Revelation 12:10–11 (*ASV*), which describes both aggressive and defensive action. "The Accuser . . . is cast down. . . . And they overcame him because of—

1. The blood of the Lamb;

2. Because of the word of their testimony;

3. Because they loved not their life even unto death."
i.e., the ground of the blood—Calvary—testified to, and *lived* in lives yielded to death.

The full equipment for the warfare depicted in Ephesians 6 is this moment-by-moment conformity to the death of Christ, and a moment-by-moment apprehension of our union with Him in the spiritual position of Ephesians 1:20–22, with Ephesians 2:6, i.e., "All things in subjection *under His feet* . . . and *raised us up with Him, and made us to sit with Him* . . . " (*ASV*). Then, "in the strength of His might," united in spirit to the ascended Lord, we are "able to stand AGAINST" the spiritual forces of the enemy, whom He defeated at Calvary.

Particulars of the magazine *The Overcomer* may be obtained from:

The Overcomer Literature Trust
9-11 Clothier Road
Brislington, Bristol
Avon, BS4 5RL, England